A Beginner's Guide to Caring for Ex-Batts

Discovering the joys of ex-commercial hens

Jo Barlow

ISBN: 148408067X
ISBN-13:978-1484080672

DEDICATION

This book is dedicated to all those hens in cages who will never experience the warmth of the sun on their feathers.

And to Audrey, Agatha and Aurora, whose unconditional love changed my life forever.

Audrey, Agatha and Aurora in the snow

Front cover: Miss Audrey Chicken three months after rehoming.
Front Cover Insert: Miss Audrey Chicken on rehoming day.
Back Cover: Miss Bunty Goodchicken

CONTENTS

ACKNOWLEDGMENTS

So many people have helped me with the writing of this book and I am eternally grateful to them all.

Special thanks to Judy Napper for her proofreading expertise and invaluable friendship, to Sophie Mccoy for her advice and support in publishing the book, to Brigit Strawbridge for her belief in me, to the wonderful Paula Adams who is my chicken angel, to Tim at poultrykeeper.com for giving me my first chickeny writing gig and consequently the confidence to actually write this book and to Lou Apted whose IT brilliance stopped me losing the plot completely.

An enormous thank you goes to all my mad chicken friends without whom I would just be a lone madwoman. Their advice and support have been invaluable during my journey into keeping ex-batts and I have learnt so much from them all. We are a wonderful group – we laugh together and we cry together. And we eat cake together. A lot of it! If caring for ex-batts has changed my life, then so has their friendship. Thank you ladies.

Thank you to my darlings, Tom and Caroline, who put up with me talking about chickens all the time, who have given up their bedrooms for sick chickens and who make me so proud every day just by being the amazing people they are.

Finally and most importantly, thank you to my long-suffering husband Gary, whose life has also been taken over by ex-batts, whether he likes it or not! Neither I nor this book would be here without him.

Miss Eliza Chicken

INTRODUCTION

My first ex-batts were really just a part of our bid to live a greener lifestyle in our new home in Cornwall. Inspired to become a little like Tom and Barbara Goode (in all honesty I was always more Margot), I had originally planned to 'just have a few hens'. Cue the arrival of Audrey, Aurora and Agatha chickens and cue the start of my most important discovery. Up until that moment I had only ever thought of ex-batts as a whole, I had never thought of them as individual girls, with characters, feelings, fears and worries.

It only took me a few moments to completely fall in love with my girls, to fall under their spell and to realise this was the start of something very important. I opened the back door and they all ran across the garden into my arms. From that moment I was a lost cause! You see, whilst I thought it was me doing the rescuing, in fact it was those first three beautiful girls with their fragile bodies, big hearts and unconditional love who rescued me. I had been ill and they had made me well. I am forever in their debt so I decided that in return I would rescue as many of their caged sisters as I could.

I now co-ordinate re-homings in Cornwall for Fresh Start for Hens and find loving homes for ex-commercial hens. I also write about my girls extensively in a bid to encourage other people to find room in their homes and their hearts for these special little hens. In my telling their stories, my girls have become successful ambassadors for their caged sisters! Audrey was a BHWT sponsor girl and Agatha and Aurora were calendar girls. Bunty Goodchicken was a magazine covergirl, is having a medical paper written about her brave fight against Egg Peritonitis and has won a Braveheart Award. Effie has a fan club, has appeared on a T-shirt and people from all over the country have come to visit her. Effie, being the consummate professional she is, is always happy to meet and greet her public, especially if they bring her a tasty treat of mealworms! Effie's eggs have even appeared on television in a programme about hen welfare, it's not every girl that can say her eggs have been made into a soufflé by a Masterchef champion! Effie, Miss Basket and Bunty Goodchicken's stories and pictures have also appeared in a museum in Los Angeles. My girls regularly feature in magazines and on websites, all the while inspiring other kind hearted souls to rehome some ex-batts.

There is so much animal cruelty in this world that I feel powerless to stop – bears being milked for their bile, beautiful dolphins and killer whales entombed in tanks for the amusement of the public, tigers killed for their body parts,, dogs mistreated and beaten – it breaks my heart. I can raise awareness and campaign but ultimately I cannot stop it happening. But I can help a few little ex-commercial hens. Rehoming ex-batts is my very small contribution towards improving the welfare of these very precious little girls. There are millions of hens in the UK and worldwide who will never see the sun or forage for worms. These little hens deserve the chance to experience the free range life every hen should be enjoying.

If you are reading this book, then hopefully offering a loving home to some ex-batts is something you are thinking of doing or are already doing. I hope you find the information in here useful and helpful as you start your ex-batt-keeping journey. However, the most important piece of advice I can give you is, to enjoy your girls. They will lift your spirits on the darkest day and they will return your love tenfold. Ex-batts are life enhancing and they provide sunshine for even the weariest soul.

My girls have taught me so much about the care and welfare of ex-batts. They have been excellent teachers, I hope I have been a competent pupil. Every single one of my ex-batts is pictured in this book and every hen featured is one of my girls. This book is really a tribute to them, so that their stories are told and their memories live on.

If you would like to read more about their tales and adventures please visit my blog: **http://lifewiththeexbatts.wordpress.com/**

Ex-batts have changed my life. They will change yours too.

Jo xx

Miss Bella Chicken

CHAPTER 1

Why Ex-Batts?

If you are new to keeping chickens or indeed thinking of adding to your existing flock, why should you chose ex-batts over some of the other more showgirly pure breeds?

Well, put very simply, you will be saving a life. Ex-commercial hens, be they caged, barn or free range, are all sent to slaughter after approximately 18 months of intensive laying as they are no longer commercially viable. This is when rehoming charities intervene and buy as many hens as they can from the farmer and then pass them on to their new loving owners.

Ex-batts will return your love tenfold. They will race across the garden to greet you, always hoping for a delicious treat. They will brighten the darkest day with their antics and their quirky personalities. You will fall in love with them and you will end up having some more.

If you are the sort of person who loves helping animals (and if you are reading this I expect that you are!) there is nothing better than taking a frightened featherless little chicken, caring for her, nurturing her and loving her and seeing her slowly beginning to do all the things her little body has been desperate to do all her life – sunbathing, scratching, foraging, preening, nesting, worm hunting. It is the most rewarding thing I have ever done and I know you will feel the same.

On a practical note, your hens will be healthy (charities will never knowingly rehome an unhealthy girl), the hens come fully vaccinated and they will provide you with delicious free range eggs.

Ask anyone who already rehomes ex-batts about their girls and you will receive an enthusiastic, and probably very long, animated response extolling the virtues of their ladies. I can guarantee, that if you do rehome some ex-batts, within days it will be you giving that enthusiastic, animated response!

Whilst ex-battery hens are just as easy to care for as any other chickens, these very special ladies do require some extra consideration and treatment after the ordeal they have been through. I hope you find the information and tips I have picked up over the years with my own beautiful ex-batts useful as you start your journey with your own special girls.

So What Exactly Are Ex-Batts?

For the purpose of this book, the term ex-batts is used to mean all ex-commercial hens.

In the UK and EU we have caged, barn and free range hens. Caged eggs make up about 50% of the market, barn eggs and organic eggs a fraction and free range approximately the other 50%.

However, with the 2012 barren cage ban now in force there is a misconception that there are no more caged hens in the UK.

Unfortunately this is not true. The ban finally saw the end of the tiny, cramped cages where each hen had less room than an A4 size piece of paper but they were replaced by enriched, and more recently colony, cages.

Caged Systems

1. Enriched Cages

These were original replacement for barren cages, giving each hen about 20% more room. Imagine that A4 piece of paper and add a postcard. The cages have nest boxes, litter, perch space and some scratching materials and house up to ten hens.

2. Colony Cages

These larger cages house 60-80 hens in large aircraft hangar-style buildings which are full of these cages. They have the same facilities as the enriched cages and the same amount of room per hen. In each cage of 80 hens there are four nest boxes.

What is Good About the New Cages?

The most important benefit of the new larger cages is that they are an acknowledgement by the egg industry that the barren cages were an inhumane way of treating commercial hens and, as such, an important step forward in the advancement of hen welfare. The new facilities give the hens the opportunity to exhibit some basic natural behaviours such as perching, scratching and nesting.

What Similarities are There to the Old Barren Cages?

Unfortunately all too many. Hens will never see natural daylight, they still stand on wire floors, they are still routinely de-beaked, they are still sent to slaughter at about 18 months. Commercial hens are bred to produce high numbers of eggs (an egg a day) for a short period of time. This depletes their body of calcium and leads to brittle bones. Movement is still restricted – remember there is only 20% more room than the barren cages - and feather pecking still occurs. Hens coming out of the new cages are in a very similar state to those coming out of the old barren ones.

Above: Lucky hens waiting for their new owners on rehoming day. Note the variation in feather coverage. Some girls are well feathered, others have hardly any. This can happen in all commercial systems where there are large flock sizes. A chicken can recognise up to 80 other hens so these girls will probably all be strangers, despite coming from the same farm.

What Problems are There With the New Cages?

There are very limited facilities in the new cages. Four nest-boxes for 80 hens is a tiny amount and will cause fighting; dominant hens will ensure hens lower in the pecking order cannot access this facility. Submissive hens will also still not be able to escape bullying. The scratching area is often artificial turf so the hen cannot properly scratch or forage, which is another basic natural behaviour. Nor can she fly, jump, preen properly, dust-bathe, sunbathe or even spread her wings. Imagine an aircraft hangar full of these cages, thousands upon thousands of chickens stacked cage upon cage. This stocking density, which is also two cages deep, makes checking for unwell hens difficult and dead hens may lie unnoticed for days. The hens are still nothing more than a faceless commodity.

Non-Caged Systems

Barn Hens

In barn systems EU regulations state there is a maximum of nine hens per square metre, comparative luxury to the A4 sized piece of paper. Hens can move around and peck, stretch their wings, scratch and lay their egg in a nest. They do not, however, ever see daylight, they are routinely debeaked, suffer from calcium deficiency-related health problems and suffer from feather pecking and bullying from other hens in a confined space with limited facilities to fight over

Free Range

Free range hens are housed in a similar way to the barn hens but must have constant access to the fresh air with outside vegetation and each hen must have at least four square metres of space. Hens will usually still have their beaks trimmed. There are also many levels of free range – it is not necessarily the ideal that the egg company marketing Svengalis lead you to believe. Hens coming out of some free range systems be as featherless as barn or caged girls although they will generally be much fitter. 'Access to the fresh air' is a suitably broad comment and can be as little as one small access hole to the outside for many thousands of hens. It is easily blocked and congestion and fighting mean many of those hens will not have access to the open air.

At the other end of the free range spectrum in organic free range systems the access is much improved and beak trimming is usually not permitted. According to Soil Association regulations, each hen has a minimum of ten square metres of outside space and only six birds per square metre are allowed inside the sheds.

One point to remember is that *all* commercial hens (yes that includes barn and free range) are sent to slaughter at 18 months. So whether the hens you rehome are from caged, barn or free range systems you will be saving a life. It can get very overwhelming seeing so much suffering and abuse of animals throughout our world and often frustrating as there is nothing we can do. But by offering a home to a few little ex-batt hens you will be saving their lives. It may be a tiny drop in a very big ocean but always remember that:

Saving one hen will not change the world but it will change the world for that hen.

Miss Audrey Chicken and Miss Agatha Chicken enjoying the sun

Miss Daisy Chicken

CHAPTER 2

Where Do You Get Ex-Batts From?

Once you have made the, quite frankly, splendid decision to rehome ex-batts where do you get them from?

I cannot stress strongly enough that you should get your ex-batts through a hen rehoming organisation. You could in theory buy them directly from the farmer but some unscrupulous farmers have become wise to the demand for ex-batts as pets and sell them to the public. This means your money goes directly into their pockets and I for one would not be responsible in any small way for funding these commercial farms. Any money you donate to rehoming organisations, however, will be invested into the future of rescuing ex-batts, promoting their terrible plight and campaigning for improved conditions for all hens. Plus you will be assured of a healthy hen, who has had her claws trimmed, and have the added reassurance of helplines and support should you need any advice.

There are numerous hen re-homing organisations who work with the farmers to intercept the chickens otherwise destined for slaughter. They also highlight the plight of the battery hen and intensive farming in general as well as raising funds to enable them to help more of the 16 million battery hens in the UK each year. Only a tiny fraction of these hens are currently rehomed and the hen rehoming organisations are crying out for more loving homes to provide these girls with the free range life they deserve.

The charities will, quite rightly, ask for a donation for the chickens. This covers vet bills, the money they pay to the farmer, transport and fuel costs, advertising, and so on and generally is somewhere between £2 and £5 per hen. As a volunteer co-ordinator I can assure you a great amount of time, money and effort is given to organising the re-homings and these donations go some way towards those costs. Larger charities like the BHWT take donations on re-homing day but some smaller organisations do ask for payment up front when you register, to avoid losing precious funds from 'no shows.'

Hen Rehoming Organisations
(for full contact details please see chapter 9)

British Hen Welfare Trust: UK wide, donations of £3-£4 per hen.

Free at Last: Based in Bedfordshire. Donations of £1.50 per hen.

Fresh Start for Hens: UK wide, including Cornwall, donations of £2.50 per hen

Little Hen Rescue: Small hen re-homing charity based in Norfolk.

Lucky Hen Rescue: Based in Wigan.

Northern Ireland Hen Rescue: Based in Northern Ireland

RSPCA: Some RSPCA branches rehome ex-batts, such as RSPCA Cornwall

Wing and a Prayer Rescue: Scotland.

Things to Consider

Before you contact the rehoming organisations and register your interest for some ex-batts there are a few things to consider. Like all pets, chickens are a commitment and it is your duty to ensure their health, happiness and safety.

How Many Chickens do You Want?

Hen rehoming organisations state that you must rehome a minimum of three chickens, as hens are flock creatures and need company. Three or four chickens fit comfortably into a standard coop and provide a 'standard' family with more than enough eggs. I started with three hens although I would normally advise having four if these are your first girls. You don't need a cockerel for a hen to lay eggs - you only need him if you want to raise chicks. Incubating and raising chicks is not something I would ever attempt to do, nor would I advise you to. It is something best left to the experienced chicken breeding experts.

Costs

Unless you are lucky enough to inherit a coop, you will need to buy a secure coop and run for your girls. Always get the best you can afford as it will be built better, be more secure and last longer. A brief internet search shows that you can buy a small coop/run for as little as £100 (probably cheaper on eBay or secondhand). Then you must add in feed, bedding, food bowls and so on. Also when they are ill, hens will need to visit the vet. Not counting the set-up costs such as a coop and run, feeders and so on, the following table is a very rough estimate of yearly costs for four chickens. Naturally prices vary and *it does not include vets bills!* I have included basic medicines and you may of course not use them all in a year.

Estimated annual cost of caring for four hens

Costs	Estimated usage	Ind cost	Per year
Bedding – Easibed	1 per month	£6.25	£75.00
Red mite powder	2 per yr	£10.00	£20.00
Louse powder	1 per yr	£10.00	£10.00
Diatom powder	1 x 2kg tub per yr	£20.00	£20.00
Mite spray	2 per year	£10.00	£20.00
Layers mash	3 sacks per year	£8.00	£24.00
Worms	0.5 tub per month	£6.00	£36.00
Corn	2 sacks per year	£8.00	£16.00
Poultry spice	1 per year	£6.00	£6.00
Garlic powder	1 per year	£5.00	£5.00
Grit	3kg per year	£1.00	£3.00
Oyster shell	3kg per year	£1.00	£3.00
ACV	1 per year	£10.00	£10.00
Limestone flour	2kg per yr	£1.00	£2.00
Nutridrops	1 per year	£7.50	£7.50
Epsom salts	1/10 per year	£3.50	£1.00
Purple spray	1 per year	£5.00	£5.00
Calpol	1 per year	£3.00	£3.00
Gloves	2 per year	£1.00	£2.00
Flubenvet	1 per year	£14.00	£14.00
Arnica	1 per year	£4.50	£4.50
Vaseline	1 per year	£3.00	£3.00
Total			**£290**

Prices are correct as at April 2013

Space

Do you have enough space for chickens? They don't require much room - a small back garden will easily be enough for three or four chickens. But are you going to keep them in the run or let them free range? There certainly isn't enough room in the run of standard commercial coops for the chickens to truly experience freedom and if you aren't happy to let them trash you garden (and they will!) a compromise may be an area of garden fenced off for their use.

Time

Chickens don't take up much time, much less than a dog who needs regular walking! However, they do need to be let out in the morning, which is OK at 8am in the winter, not so good at 5.30am in the summer. They also need to be locked up before dusk, which can be 4pm in the winter. If you aren't at home at this time, will they be in a secure run and safe from predators? Their coops need de-pooing each morning which takes 10 minutes and cleaning out properly once a week, which takes about an hour. Plus you need to keep food and water topped up daily. You could spend as little as 15 minutes a day caring for your chickens although personally I can happily spend hours! And what about if you go away on holiday? Do you have a friend who can house-sit? Hen hotels are now popping up all over the country although this can be expensive if you have lots of girls.

Once you have considered all these facts and decided you can give a wonderful home to some precious girls please visit the websites listed in Chapter 9 and find a hen rehoming organisation with a collection point near you and register your interest.

Little Girls With Big Personalities!

One very important thing to consider when getting ex-batts is that they will take over your life and steal your heart. If someone had told me before I had hens that they were all very different, that they all had characters, I would have laughed! But it is true. Audrey was a prime example of this. Featherless and intrepid from the start, she was the first to have a dustbath in a plant pot, the first to associate the spade with worms (as soon as she saw it she became your shadow,) and the first (and so far only) girl to work the catflap. The three A girls used to take dustbaths together and when I called them their heads would emerge from their dusty ablutions, like three shower-capped old ladies, indignant at being interrupted! Audrey was also top hen until the arrival of Bella!

The first night Bella arrived she attacked the other hens, she attacked me, she attacked Gary and she attacked her own reflection (they were in the greenhouse). She was really just a frightened little hen. The next day she calmed down and very quickly became top hen, ousting Audrey from her pedestal, although Audrey was allowed to be lady-in-waiting.

Bertha and Brigit were two very beautiful blonde Amberlink girls but never were there a pair of grumpier, Victor Meldrew-esque hens! On the arrival and consequent introduction of the C girls, they both took agin poor limpy Clara and therefore spent much time in the Naughty Coop thinking about their actions. Then there was gentle Bunty Goodchicken, the original Goodchicken sister and the sweetest girl who became a medical pioneer, a BraveHeart Award winner and a magazine covergirl!

Clara liked to be picked up even after her legs were better. She used to sit in the coop, wings almost outstretched, saying 'Pick me up Mum.' CocoChanel liked to lay her eggs in the hedge and I have lost count of the number of times our neighbour discovered me crawling through it to retrieve Coco!

Little Daisy Doos came home from my first rescue and had an obsession with feet. She used to climb onto them and go to sleep. Dolly blossomed after her implant and became such a happy girl, resplendent in her new set of strawberry blonde feathers.

Effie and Miss Basket, two special little girls who came with such physical and emotional problems they spent three months inside the house in a special ICU receiving extra care, are friends and sisters. They go everywhere together, and especially love to sleep in a two-hen pyramid formation at night in their little bespoke coop. Eliza makes such a fuss about finding a delicious treat that by the time she has finished chirping about it, someone else has stolen it.

Grace Kelly loves her baths – she bwarks away contentedly and fans out her feathers during her blow dry whilst Greta Garbo, the kindhearted girl who cleans everyone else's beaks, is just so happy in her new life that her joy is contagious!

Miss Brigit Chicken

Miss Agatha Chicken

CHAPTER 3

Getting Ready – The Coop and Run

So your girls are reserved and now the all-important preparation can begin in earnest!

Coop and Run

First You Need a Secure Coop

Security is the main priority, followed closely by comfort. It needs to be well ventilated but not draughty. Air holes at the top of the coop will draw the air upwards, keeping it well ventilated, but air holes lower down will only cause draughts. There needs to be sufficient nest boxes for the hens, as well as perches. You may well find the ex-batts will not perch, but they need to have the option. In my main coop, the luxurious Henderlay, I have five nestboxes and currently five hens although I have had up to nine hens in there. If you are buying a coop, remember that manufacturers are stingy with regard to size. If they state that a coop is big enough for six to eight hens, it will be fine for three to four. Your girls have spent enough time cramped in a cage, so spend as much as you can afford on comfortable accommodation. I have also found the catches and locks on commercial coops to be flimsy so replace these with more sturdy ones of your own.

Wood or Plastic?

Coops can either be plastic or wood. Wood looks prettier, is usually cheaper and, being a natural product, breathes but it is harder to clean, takes longer to dry and can harbour red mite. Plastic can look less attractive, is more expensive but is quick to clean and all but eliminates the risk of red mite (see Chapter 6). I have both and on reflection, slightly prefer the plastic but am quite happy with the wooden ones, our beautiful custom made Henderlay (below) is wood.

Henderlay has a high coop. This makes it much more fox proof and an easy height to clean out. It stands on concrete slabs to prevent foxes digging under the wire. The ramp, however, is quite steep so not ideal for girls with poorlie legs. We have lined it with an old piece of lino which is easy to remove and clean each week. If I had it built again I would make the run twice the size.

Whilst a good height for the hens and for us to walk into, it is too small should I want to lock the girls away for any length of time. It has a clear plastic cover on top of the run, made from two plastic corrugated sheets from B&Q - about £4 each but very effective.

Prices vary, but as with everything buy the best you can reasonably afford. Commercial wooden coops for four hens retail from about £100 but are cheaper if you buy them secondhand or on eBay. Plastic coops for the same number of hens retail from about £250, again they are cheaper secondhand. Or try freecycle for a free coop that only needs a little tlc to restore it to its former glory.

Left: Our first coop. Cheap with a homemade run (minus the door we forgot and had to add later!) This run is still going strong and now has had a tarpaulin cover added. The coop has not worn well though. As a starter coop for three hens it was OK, but there are better options available.

Above: Our second coop. Cheap and ideal for three hens. Easy to assemble and clean. With this size run they would need to be free ranging most of the day. I found the perch was very flimsy and needed replacing, as did the locks on the door and nestbox.

The Cluckbuddy plastic coop. I have one for Effie and Miss Basket. Mine is a prototype for the ones that are now on sale (see stockists in Chapter 9). Effie and Miss Basket trialled it for the manufacturers and I wrote a review on it. It is designed for three ex-batts, and Effie, Miss Basket and I love it! It is white as this keeps costs down, at £250 it is at the lower end of the plastic coop market. Being plastic it takes a few minutes to clean out. We have put our old run from the original coop onto it. *Picture by kind permission of http://cluckbuddy.com*

However, you do not need to make a large investment. Is there a shed you can convert? Or a child's plastic playhouse? You can make nest boxes out of plastic crates or maybe cat carriers. As long as it is secure, warm and dry I can assure you the hens will not mind! When we had our coop built, there were not enough nestboxes (in my overfussy opinion) so we cut up two plastic lettuce crates and they make wonderful nestboxes! They are easy to clean and the girls all pile in there at night quite happily.

Ask to see a friend's coop so you can see how they are set up, what works for them and what you think would be best for you and your new girls.

The Run
Here you have two options. You can either have them in a coop with a large run that they stay in, with a little supervised free ranging at times, or you can have them in a coop and smaller run and let them free range during the day, the run just being for security in the early morning and evenings.

Coop and Large Run

Left: A beautiful coop and large run. Many thanks to the lovely Jan Webb for the photo.

This picture shows an ideal set-up. The girls have a secure coop within the run which provides additional security at night. The run is large enough for the girls with plenty to entertain them. There is shelter (from sun and rain), shade and greenery (hens feel secure when under foliage – they originate from jungle fowl) and a dustbath area. An old tyre filled with dirt is good for this, or a child's sandpit, even a large shallow flowerpot. There are perches and various levels to add interest and allow hens lower in the pecking order to escape any unwanted pecks. There is scratching material to keep them busy; a handful of grain thrown down will keep them happily occupied for hours.

Coop and Small Run and Free Ranging
This is my option of choice. I feel the girls have spent enough time cooped up (sorry!) and deserve as much freedom as I can give them. That said, we have a very secure garden and I am able to be at home much of the day. If the girls are only going to be in the run first and last thing it does not have to be enormous, just as long as they have plenty of room to move about, eat their mash and so on.

It is vital to ensure your garden is as safe as it can be from predators. Make sure all fences are secure and hole free to prevent foxes getting in and inquisitive chickens getting out. Electric fencing is a marvellous option to keep Mr Fox out, although not a cheap one. I cannot stress how important it is to make your garden as secure from any predators as you can. It would be a tragedy to rescue your little hens from slaughter and then to lose them to the fox.

Other things in the garden to be aware of are ponds (especially if frozen over!), wood piles (make a great climbing frame to the nearest fence), water butts, gates – ensure they are locked and poisonous plants that need removing. Some of the most common ones are buttercups, clovers, daffodils, delphiniums, elderberry, foxglove, hemlock, lily-of-the-valley, tuilps and rhododendron.

Hens will instinctively avoid these plants anyway – I have some of them in my garden – but if possible move them away from your girls.

In short, imagine you have a small child in the garden and envisage any dangers they may encounter!!

However, if your girls are given free run of the garden they will trash it. To oblivion! So fence off any precious plants or veggies. A fence made of chicken wire is a cheap and easy way of keeping your girls and your garden safe.

Your garden will naturally have shade, greenery and scratching areas and much to keep your girls busy but make sure you set aside an old flower bed for a dustbath. Ours use the greenhouse for a dustbath, much to the detriment of the plants! We have also built a little rainy day shelter out of an old fence panel, turned on its side and propped up against the wall.

Security

I am harping on I know but I am paranoid about foxes, badgers, dogs and so on. Your girls are precious and vulnerable. There are many tips to deter these predators and I have listed some of them in the hope that one or two of them are do-able in your situation.

- Foxes have been known to scale six-foot-high fences so the higher the fence the better.

- If building your own run, dig down and bury the fencing a foot down. Foxes will not usually be able to dig down that far.

- Use a wire skirt around the edges of the run. Alternatively lay concrete or stones around the edge, the foxes will not be able to work out that they have to start digging further back.

- Security lighting may only deter them a little but will at least advertise their arrival to you.

- Playing the radio (Radio 4 is good as there is a lot of talking) in the garden will make the fox think there is a human in the garden.

- Male urine around the perimeters will 'mark' the territory.

- I am currently resisting the urge to put a baby monitor in the coop... Just!

Bedding

There are many alternatives. I line the coop and nestboxes with newspaper and top up with bedding. I started with sawdust on the coop floor and straw in the nestboxes. However, I found the straw can harbour red mites, was tricky to clean out and could trigger allergies so now I use Easibed, which is a compostable eco-friendly horse bedding that is more comfortable for the hens and easier to clean as well as not being a harbourer of red mites. There is also Easichick as well as a hemp based product called Hemcore which are both equally good. I also put a little straw on top for extra warmth and for the hens to nest in – they instinctively throw straw or long grass over their backs before they lay an egg. Daisy Doos used to walk around with what appeared to be half a bush on her back!! I poo pick every morning before the egg laying rush and replace all bedding once a week.

Coop Hygiene
Ex-batts can pick up red mite from wild birds and they can also catch lice. To prevent this invest in some louse powder and red mite powder to dust your girls with. Depending on the brand, they can either be used on the girls or the coop so check the label carefully.

Also invest in some Diatom powder for the coop. It can be bought in large 2kg tubs which will last a year or so and is a completely natural product. Poultryshield is one brand of coop disinfectant that I have found effective as it also removes the waxy coating on red mite causing them to dehydrate and die.

If you are not confident handling your girls at first you can put the powders in their dustbath and they will dust themselves!
After I have cleaned the coop I leave it to dry, then liberally dust with diatom powder. I then line with newspaper, put in the bedding and then dust the bedding with a little more diatom and red mite powder. Obviously in the winter, as with all other bitey bugs, this is not such a priority but come the spring and warmer months, it is very important that you keep on top of any nasties. As another line of defence against the dreaded red mite, I usually spray the coop after disinfecting it with a red mite killer, such as Johnsons, every few weeks during the summer months.

Miss Basket Chicken

CHAPTER 4

Getting Ready – Food Supplements and First Aid

In the farm your girls will have eaten dry layers mash so stock up on this. If you try to feed anything different they may not recognise it and consequently may not eat it. If you want to change to pellets at a later date then introduce them slowly once your girls have settled in. Personally I am very happy with layers mash - I usually dampen it down with cold water in the summer and warm in the winter.

Ex-batts will need constant access to their food as well as fresh water. Both food and water need to be changed daily.

Chickens do not have teeth so they need grit added to their food to help grind it up in their crops. Either they can have a separate bowl available at all times or you can add a large pinch each day to their foods. Girls free ranging in the garden will probably pick up enough grit in their foraging but it is best to have extra for them.

There are a vast variety of feeders and drinkers on the market – of all different sizes, shapes and materials. I prefer Mason Cash dog bowls for food and drink. They are heavy so they cannot be kicked over and are long lasting. The only drawbacks are that the girls sometimes kick dirt into the water bowl or stand in it with their pooey feet. Food and water will therefore need changing every day.

Supplements
The shops are teeming with wonder products to help your girls but start with:

Poultry spice and garlic powder
For immunity

Limestone flour
To restore calcium levels. Put a pinch of each in their food each day.

Apple cider vinegar is a fabulous product for hens! It helps keeps worms at bay, is a good overall general conditioner, stops candida growth and helps your girls relax. Hens hate change in their routine and the rehoming will have been very stressful for them. They also love the taste!

First Aid

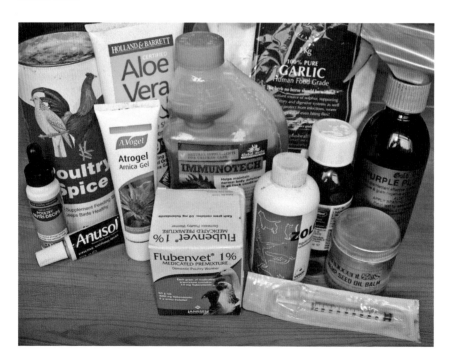

I will deal with ex-batt ailments in detail in Chapter 6, but just as with children, it is better to be ready for any illness! Once again the shop shelves are overflowing with a scary amount of seemingly essential products.

The first aid kit is something you can build as you need to but to start with I would suggest:

Calpol (2months +) - for pain relief. Give 1ml per kg of body weight of your hen, after food. Ex-batts weigh approximately 2kg. It has to be the Calpol 2months though. As with all pain relief it is to be used with caution and only if absolutely necessary.
Purple spray – an essential antiseptic spray to cover red areas and stop them from being pecked.
Hibiscrub - a general antiseptic wash for wounds.
Arnica – gel or cream, it treats sore legs and bruising effectively and quickly.
Nutridrops – especially good during the moult and to promote a dwindling appetite.
Vaseline – for pecked combs and also to lubricate the vent if necessary.
Flubenvet – the only licensed wormer for hens in the UK. You can also eat the eggs during treatment.
Critical Care Formula – dissolve 1 tablespoon of honey in a litre of boiled water and a few grains of both salt and citric acid. For hens who are not eating or drinking.
Honey - for shrinking prolapses. Also use as a general addition to food or water to aid health.
Salt - for bathing wounds.
Disposable gloves
Syringes - save the 1ml and 2ml syringes issued with prescription medicine.

Also ensure you have a place you can put your sick hen — a spare coop, a cat carrier in the kitchen or, in the case of our Effie, the spare bedroom. Keep her warm and dry with access to food and water and tempt her with treats such as scrambled egg if necessary.

But, the single most important thing you can do for the health and welfare of your ex-batts is to find a good chicken vet. Until very recently, hens were classed as livestock and treated as such; for example a couple of chickens would be culled to diagnose the illness and then the rest of the flock would treated. However, you would no more 'cull' your sick pet chicken than you would your sick family dog.

Many vets are realising this and organisations such as Chicken Vet run courses for vets and have an ever-growing list of associated practices across the UK:
http://www.chickenvet.co.uk/associated-practices/

Picking Up an Ex-batt

Before I had my first girls I had never picked up a chicken so asked a friend at work if I could practise on his hens! If you have never picked up a hen, it is good to try to get some experience as your new girls will not be used to human contact and will probably protest loudly about being picked up, as well as trying to avoid it at all costs.

Stand behind the hen (it is good to distract her with some corn or other tasty treat) and bring your hands together gently but firmly round the widest part of her body. Pick her up, holding her wings firmly into her body. She will try to flap and there is little more painful than a wing slap in the face! More importantly she may injure herself! She may struggle so hold her firmly but gently until she quietens down. If you do not have a good grip, place her back on the floor, readjust your grip and pick her up again.

Top Chicken Bella tolerating a cuddle

Once she is quiet bring her into your body so one side of her is nestling into you. This frees up one hand and you can support her under her chest and abdomen with the other whilst still keeping your thumb firmly over that wing! That free hand can always be used to cradle her a little more firmly if she starts to try and wiggle free.

If you struggle with this at first, you can try wrapping her in a towel (leaving her head and neck poking out) and picking her up that way.

Whilst all ex-batty people love chicken cuddles, there is a serious side to them. Firstly you become more confident in handling your hens and secondly your hens become used to being handled. This makes regular checks easier for you, and much less stressful for the hen and, should they need to go to the vet, the whole experience is much less traumatic for all involved.

Cuddling Girl Miss Clara Chicken

Chicken Cuddling Wednesday

As part of a jolly twitter campaign I started Chicken Cuddling Wednesday to encourage people to cuddle their hens more often. I chose Wednesday because we all need cheering up from that midweek slump. Some hens love being cuddled, others are convinced you are trying to kill them. My big, blonde, beautiful Clara was my cuddling girl. We used to sing My Favourite Things together, my reedy warblings complemented by Clara's perfectly pitched bwarks:

Raindrops on roses and feathers on chickens
Bright copper kettles and warm woollen mittens
Brown paper packages tied up with string
Clara is one of my favourite things
Chickens in white feathers with blue satin sashes
Doorbells and sleighbells and Clara with eyelashes
Clara who flies with the moon on her wings
Clara is one of my favourite things.

Clara loved her cuddle and she loved her song, even if I was singing it by myself in the garden, she would skip up to me and join in. Since my darling Clara passed away in her sleep I have tried to sing it on my own but it just makes me too sad. It is not the same without her.

Portrait of Cuddling Girl Clara painted by the very talented and lovely Janet Jamieson.

Miss Greta Garbo Chicken

CHAPTER 5

Bringing Your Girls Home

Just before the rehoming you will receive confirmation from the co-ordinator and suddenly it will all become real! The Big Day is fast approaching and your ex-batts will soon be arriving!

Big Day Checklist

Ensure the coop is clean, diatom poofed and made up with bedding
Have food and water containers full and ready in the run
Have louse powder and Vaseline to hand
Carriers and boxes should be lined with paper and bedding and in the car!
Make sure that details of location and time are also in the car – you would be amazed how many people get lost!
The co-ordinator's phone number – see above!

The Journey to a New Life

Remember that whilst it is a Big Day for you, it is an even bigger one for your girls. Up until that day, their lives will have consisted of a wire cage with no natural sunlight or fresh air. Absolutely everything they encounter from now on will be new and scary! I have found cat carriers lined with newspaper and bedding are a secure, easy way to transport your new girls. Two hens fit into one large cat carrier snugly, but are not too cramped. If you do not have cat carriers, sturdy cardboard boxes with postbox style slits for ventilation will be just fine. Take some parcel tape to seal them up.

Personally I have found that taking an extra person along is very helpful as they can sit in the back of the car with the new chickens and keep an eye on them. This stops me casting furtive glances round every few minutes to check on them. Also, newly freed ex-batts have a dreadful smell, so open the driver's window!

When your girls get home, as you take them out dust them with louse powder and put Vaseline on their combs, then pop them gently into the run with the coop pophole open and let them explore their new world. Newly freed ex-batts will have no fear and may wander off so they need to stay in their coop and run until their home is imprinted on them. They have no knowledge of night and day having been exposed to 18 hours of artificial light so will need encouragement to go into their coop at dusk. This is another reason to keep them confined to their run at first!

They will eat a great deal at first, but don't be alarmed. Once they realise that the food is readily available they will settle into eating just what they need.

Miss Aurora Chicken on Rehoming Day

Their legs may be weak from lack of use so try and make the ramp less steep by making it longer. Use another piece of wood or even prop it on a sturdy stone if it appears too steep. Alternatively, physically put them in the coop each night until they are steadier on their legs. Rub their legs with arnica gel or cream to help them.

They have no experience of perching and at first the perch can actually get in the way, so remove it from the coop until their legs are stronger. Once they are hopping in and out of the coop and nest box, pop it back in as chickens naturally want to perch. That said, none of mine have ever mastered it and tuck up snugly in the nest box together at night!

Your girls will have come from a temperature controlled environment so will need to be kept warm or cool as necessary. Make sure the coop is draught free and bedding is extra soft, as sore pecked skin needs extra care.

Cover part of the run so they have shelter from the sun and rain They will obviously be unaware of weather and will stand out in the rain, oblivious, at first if not protected. Also that naked skin is very delicate and will burn easily, so shade from the sun is just as important.

The Pecking Order

Your little ex-batts have had a pretty rough ride through life so far and the odds are that the fewer feathers they have, the rougher that ride was. So introducing them all to each other will be quite a trauma for them. Your little flock will be strangers to each other and they will naturally establish a pecking order. This can seem quite a brutal process but too much human intervention can sometimes prolong it.

There are, however, a few things that you can do to help it along:

Pop them all in the coop together when they are asleep, so that they wake up together. We had one chicken, Bella, who was the very devil that first night. She had to be separated from the others, went to sleep in a cat box and we put her in the coop once they were all asleep. The next day there were minor skuffles but nothing too dramatic. Bella is now top chicken and very protective of her 'girls.'

Put Vaseline on the combs of all the hens so the dominant hen can't get a grip. Chickens are attracted by blood so you want to avoid that. Make sure there are plenty of feeders and drinkers around so the dominant hen doesn't hog them. Hang up some tasty greens for them to peck at to keep them occupied. Sometimes a human finger tapped (gently but firmly) on the back of the bossier hen can establish you as top chicken. This isn't 100% successful, but worth a shot! Use your anti-peck spray to cover any bleeding patches or sore red bits.

If you have a hen who is being bullied, remove the bully, NOT the bullied hen. Keep her in sight of the other hens, ideally in an adjoining coop and run. This puts her on the back foot, whilst giving the bullied hen a chance to gain both confidence and friends. Return the bully to the flock and see how she gets on. If she starts bullying again, remove her again and so on until all is calm.

Generally your hens will settle down quite quickly, alliances will form and some will develop into friendships.

Sisters, Sisters, Never Were There Such Devoted Sisters...

Any ex-batt owner will tell you that these girls can form special friendships.Effie and Miss Basket are two splendid examples of this. These two fragile girls, initially very wary of each other, soon settled into a gentle companionship which blossomed into a true and very touching friendship; a genuine love of each other. Now inseparable, the girls pootle around their half of the garden; they eat together, dust bathe together, preen each other, take turns sleeping on top of each other, run the gauntlet to the back door together and terrorise the cats together. Recently Effie has come back into lay and they sit side by side in the nest box (I imagine them chatting and clasping their knitting to their chests) but when Effie lays her egg, it is Miss Basket that comes rushing out of the coop, proudly announcing the fact!

Effie and Miss Basket, friends and sisters

But it is not just these two girls. When Bertha was ill, Bunty, Brigit and Bella took it in turns to sit with her and when she suffered her heart attack it was a very distressed Bunty that came running out of the coop to tell us. And my first ever girls – Agatha and Aurora were very close friends - allies against the dominant diva Audrey. When Aurora was ill, Aggie stayed with her the whole time and when Aurora passed away, Aggie went downhill very quickly, dying three weeks later - of a broken heart I believe.

Clara and Bunty were great friends. Both older girls, both unwell, they spent much time together in the greenhouse, resting and chatting. When Bunty finally succumbed to her illness, Clara passed away very unexpectedly three days later. Maybe life without her friend proved to be unbearable.

Their heartbreak highlights the downside of having a special friend, but, as the saying goes, it is better to have loved and lost than never to have loved at all.

Ex-Batts and Other Animals

Don't be fooled by their frail stature, ex-batts are very capable of looking after themselves when faced with a family cat. My six cats (and four feral farm cats) are all terrified of the ex-batts and slink past them - Audrey Chicken thoroughly enjoyed a game of 'chase the cat!' Effie waits by the back door to see who dares come out of the catflap! I would however, take much more time introducing a family dog to the ex-batts and never have him/her off lead in the garden until you are completely sure of their reactions.

I include children in this section as well! Ex-batts are the most amazing educators for children (and adults). Children become aware of where their food comes from – collecting eggs is a great treat - and they feel the benefits of caring for another creature. Caring for ex-batts also highlights the evils of intensive farming in their minds, something they will hopefully carry forward into their adult years. Bella Chicken came into college with me to help give a talk to the students on animal welfare. A group of teenagers who had previously scoffed at the idea of caring about chickens were enchanted by the charismatic Bella (a true spokeswoman for her girls) and horrified by her story. They were all converted and still ask about her to this day!

The Big Wide World

Once your girls have found their feet, they will be ready to explore the rest of their new world! If you have decided they are to free range in the garden, let them do so under supervision for brief spells so you can watch for any escape attempts or any potential problems. Should anyone want to spread their wings I have covered wing clipping in Chapter 6. It isn't as scary as it sounds!!

Garden Helpers

Once your girls have discovered the joys of free ranging, they will want to help you in the garden! They love nothing more than helping with the digging and eating any worms that emerge (watch that spade blade though)! Turning over the compost heap is a much anticipated treat! Even though they may be a little over-zealous in their 'help' hens are actually very good for the garden. Their poo is the best fertiliser of any animal dung and, once rotted in with the compost, will provide excellent fertile organic matter. They will prepare new beds for you, scratching through and aerating the soil, ridding it of grubs and bugs and fertilising it as they do so. Any old beds with weeds or gone over plants will be gleefully pounced upon and worked over in a matter of minutes.

Security (again!)

Always remember that if your girls are free ranging you need to be around to put them into the run before dusk to avoid any predators. In mid-winter this can be as early as 4am, in mid-summer it can be 9.30pm so always make sure you or someone else can lock them away.

As the evenings change with the seasons, so do the mornings. I can happily manage a 7.30am wake up to feed the hens in the winter - 5.30am in the summer is not so appealing. Automatic door openrs are available (the automatic opener, the door, the timer etc retail for approximately £150 all in) and will fit most standard coops. Friends use them and swear by them, although personally I prefer to count my girls in last thing at night and out first thing in the morning. I worry that if someone was having a late evening snack, mentioning no names Miss Flavia Chicken, they would get locked out and I would go and check it anyway which defeats the object!

Worming

Soon after rehoming it is advisable to worm your girls. Flubenvet is currently the only licensed wormer for hens in the UK and you can eat the eggs whilst they are being treated. It is very simple to use. Each scoop (which is provided) is 6g. Mix this very well with 2kg of food to ensure that it is evenly distributed. Your hens then need to eat this food for seven days. This kills the worm cycle. If they run out of food, make up another batch. After seven days, throw away any unused food. If you check their poo during this time - you may see the odd dead worm (looks like a bit of spaghetti). This shows the Flubenvet is working. After their initial worming, your girls will need to be wormed every three months. If you notice any wormy poos before the three months are up, they can be treated sooner.

Adding to Your Flock

Miss Aurora Chicken with feathers growing back

If you have had four girls as a first foray into ex-batt keeping and lose one, it is time to start thinking about adding at least another couple of girls to your flock. What you are trying to avoid is having one hen left. Hens are flock creatures and a solitary hen will be unhappy and not thrive. Contact your local co-ordinator and see if they have any girls available. Sometimes they have taken on poorlie girls and nursed them back to health and they will be ready for rehoming. Speaking as a co-ordinator I am all too happy to help a loving owner increase their flock. At the very least the co-ordinator will be able to tell you when the next rehoming is. Although they insisted on a minimum of three hens at your first rehoming, now you already have hens you will be able to reserve two. Although three is better!!

Integrating Your Hens!

Effie and Miss Basket, living proof that everyone can find a friend

To me this is one of the most stressful times of hen keeping. After your first girls, you will undoubtedly want some more to increase your flock and save a few more lives. But just as when you were introducing your original flock to each other there were handbags and fisticuffs, so there may well be when you introduce new girls to your established flock.

Ideally you need to have a separate coop and run or area of the garden for your new hens where they can see the old girls through a fence. They will need to be settled in just as your original girls were. They need to recover their fitness and grow in confidence. Imagine arriving in a new place, with new girls in your new house and to be faced by a gang of big, beautiful feathered girls who do not really want you there! I'd be scared.

So allow them time to see each other through the fence and get used to the sight of each other. After a couple of weeks you can bite the bullet and let them all in together to see what happens. Always do this under supervision, especially if you have a weaker hen or an obvious bully!

You can also put them all in the coop together at night when everyone is asleep. In theory everyone wakes up together, smelling the same, are suitably confused and get along.

If you have one particular bully you can apply the same trick as before, by isolating her.

I have found a slowly, slowly approach works best for me. After their initial few weeks' isolation, allow the girls to all mix in a large area for a short time. This allows any picked on hens to escape trouble. Supervise this (it is best to do this when you have a weekend or a few days off). Slowly increase their time together until you are happy everyone is calm. I leave both coops open for a while so the new girls have a refuge at night but once I am happy harmony is reigning I let them all go to bed together in one coop.

I have integrated many flocks, and sometimes just one girl into an established flock and this has been the most successful method for me and my girls.

A Cautionary Tale – Audrey's First Night

Many years ago I picked up my first ever group of ex-batts – Audrey, Agatha and Aurora. It was a much anticipated, scary and exciting day!
It was the first time I had seen chickens just out of the farm and the sight of these featherless, frightened souls taking their first tentative steps to freedom reduced me to tears. To think that so many battery hens look like this and that these are the lucky ones. These girls had loving homes waiting for them.

The relatively well-feathered Agatha was handed to me first, then came Aurora who was semi-feathered and then finally Audrey who had very few, poor darling. The girls were tucked up in their cat carrier and we made the journey home with the windows open wide – ex-batts do have a certain 'aroma' about them. So worried was I about these precious bundles that I made my daughter sit in the back seat with them and check on them every five minutes.

Audrey, Aggie and Aurora arrived to the luxury of their little coop in the back garden and spent much of that first evening just looking, taking it in. I showed them the sky and explained the green stuff was grass and that the strange smell was fresh air. Agatha stayed in the coop and rearranged the nest box and Aurora followed the intrepid oven-ready Audrey (shades of things to come) to explore the run.

That first night I was wide awake worrying about my new girls being attacked. Was the coop safe enough? Was there a fox lurking? Could the fox unlock the door? Did he have some sort of tunnelling device? Was there a gang of foxes lurking on the street corner, planning a raid on my henhouse?

So at first light I nervously trotted down the garden to open up the coop. Just two girls came out for their breakfast so I peered in the back door to check on the errant Audrey, only to be greeted by the sight of Audrey lying motionless and flat on her back with her feet in the air. Being the brave soul I am, I ran sobbing to Gary, saying that Audrey was dead. Less than 24 hours with a chicken and I had failed her and she had died. She would miss out on all that wonderful free range happiness I had planned for her; worm hunts, dustbaths, sun bathing, scratching for bugs, cuddles...

As I watched, weeping, from the safety of the lounge, Gary took Audrey's lifeless form out of the coop, placing her gently in a cardboard box. As he bent down to lock the coop door, an indignant head appeared from inside the box and bwarked loudly at him.

Moral Of The Story: *Chickens can fall over when fast asleep and stay asleep quite happily whilst still on their backs. Until rudely awakened.*

Miss Audrey Chicken taking her first ever dustbath. I never liked those pansies anyway!

Miss Dolly Chicken

CHAPTER 6

Ex-Batt Health and Wellbeing

Identifying the signs of illness in your hen and knowing how to treat her correctly is something that can seem rather daunting to an inexperienced chicken keeper. Hens are notoriously difficult to diagnose; as a predated species they hide illness until it is often too late.

Make a point of checking your hens often so you know what a healthy hen looks and feels like.

The Common Signs of a Healthy Hen:
Crop should be empty in the morning and full at night, when it should feel like one of those rice-filled stress balls - firm but not hard and yielding to gentle pressure but not squishy.
Abdomen should be firm but not hot, swollen or squishy.
Comb should be red.
Knickers and vent are clean.
Vent is pulsating normally (imagine an aged aunt pursing her lips over an unwanted swearword).
Eyes and nose are clear.
Breathing is normal.
She is alert and her tail is up.

She is eating and drinking normally.
She is active – foraging, dustbathing preening and if she is dozing in the sunshine she is looking relaxed and happy.

Miss Agatha Chicken, the picture of health!

The Common Signs Of A Sick Hen:
A hunched stance and her tail down.
Her wings trailing a little (imagine that droopy feeling you get when you feel ill).
Feathers fluffed up.
Pale comb.
Dirty bottom.
Not eating or drinking.
Sleepy.
Lack of interest in her surroundings.
She may stay in the coop or stand in a corner, facing inwards.

Poor moulty Clara, showing some of the signs of feeling unwell

If you observe your girls closely and regularly you will be able to pick up on these signs very quickly. I am normally initially alerted if one of them does not charge across the garden to see me demanding food! Mostly they are just busy doing something else far more important such as digging a hole, but sometimes it can be the very first indicator that something is not 100%.

When your hen shows symptoms of being unwell, give her a thorough check over and refer to a reliable source of information such as the Poultrykeeper Diseases page: **http://poultrykeeper.com/poultry-diseases/**. The rehoming organisations also have forums or Facebook pages you can ask for advice on. But if you are on a forum be prepared for conflicting opinions! Also be prepared for idiotic comments from non-ex-batty people about chicken sandwiches and K*C. If I had a pound for every moron that has made this 'joke' I would be a very rich woman and spend that money on running an animal sanctuary! Ignore them, they are not worth getting upset over.

Checklist

Checking her over gently and carefully, look for any immediate issues such as bleeding or obvious signs of parasites, broken legs or wings and so on. Then inspect her more closely.

Knickers: Are they clean or is there poo on them? If they are dirty have you wormed her recently?

Poo: Is it normal or is something different? You can tell a great deal about your girls' health by their poo. This webpage, from www.allotment.org.uk, is a marvellous guide to all things poo: **http://chat.allotment.org/index.php?topic=17568.0**

Vent: Is it pulsating normally or is there anything sticking out? Tissue paper-like substance sticking out may be the skin of a soft shelled egg (see P55) and can be removed by slowly pulling it out very gently. Is there a fleshy mass protruding? This may be a prolapse (see P58).

Legs: Can she walk or stand up? Is she limping? (see P61). Are the scales on her legs flakey and coming away? This may be scaly leg (see P61).

Crop: Is it hard first thing? This may be impacted crop (see P65). Is it squishy and fluidy with a foul smell? This may be sour crop (see P65).

Breathing: Is it wheezy or rattly? Is she sneezing or coughing? Are her eyes foamy? These are all symptoms of respiratory problems (see P63).

The problem may be something simple that you are happy to deal with. However – and I cannot stress this strongly enough – if you are at all unsure and require assistance or need advice then please speak to your vet and take your girl in immediately. Small animal consultation fees are about £15-£20. This is a small price to pay for your girl's health!

Also if it is your first visit to the vet ask them to show you how to administer medicines to your girls.

As your hen-keeping skills increase, you will become more adept at treating them yourself, but a good vet is always necessary to perform complicated procedures and operations and prescribe medicines for your girls as well as being a source of advice and support.

Prevention

Miss Gina Chicken in her deluxe hospital accommodation

Prevention is better than cure so ensure that you worm your girls regularly and add supplements to their feed - such as poultry spice, garlic and limestone flour.
I have already detailed a well-stocked first aid kit that will cover most eventualities but over time I would also add:

Zolcal D - a strong calcium supplement; 2ml will induce an egg bound hen's contractions to help her pass her egg. Never overdose on calcium supplements though!

Pile cream – for shrinking prolapses.

Epsom salts - dissolve a teaspoon in a cup of water, give 5ml of this solution to flush out a hen with sour crop after draining the crop.

Probiotic eg Beryl's Friendly Bacteria. This replaces good bacteria, especially after antibiotics. You could also use live yoghurt but in moderation as hens are lactose intolerant.

Bathing Your Girl

Often a warm bath is the first step when treating a sick hen. The positive effects of a warm bath cannot be over emphasised. Warmth is a great healer and it also allows you to give your girl a thorough check over whilst relaxing her and helping with pain relief if necessary. A bath can however be for something as minor as having dirty knickers. And a girl should always have clean knickers! Dirty knickers can be a sign of illness or of worms but a girl with permanently dirty knickers is at risk from fly strike. Attracted by the poo, flies lay their eggs in the feathers and the maggots will eat away at your girl's skin. It is a horrible thing and to be avoided at all costs. But bathing your girl is usually a pleasurable experience for you both – I sing to my girls when they are in the bath!

Fill a sink or large bowl with baby bath temperature water (the elbow water-testing trick comes back into play here!) and a couple of drops of lavender oil. After her initial flapping protests, your hen should stand quite still. This is often a good time to have a general check over as well. Once clean, wrap her in a towel and dry her gently. Then using a hair drier on the coolest setting, blow dry her knickers. You will be surprised how many girls love having warm air wafted around their knickers!

Ailments

Ex-batts are as easy to care for as other hens but the toll of their commercial lives means they can be more susceptible to certain conditions. Whilst the list below looks long and scary I have tried to cover all my experiences with hens, including all the information I think you might need. If your hens are anything like mine they will fall ill at 6pm on the Friday of a bank holiday weekend. Being able to treat her until you can get veterinary attention may make all the difference. If all else fails and you have to wait for the vet, keep your girl warm and comfortable and separate from her sisters. Warmth and tender loving care are great healers of hens.

Common ailments and conditions are put together in related groups which are listed below in no particular order of importance or severity!

Eggy Issues

Egg laying varies from hen to hen - I have many ex-batts who produce a perfect egg every day and a couple who never really got started! But to me, eggs are an added bonus to rehoming ex-batts. They may stop laying after a week or two due to the stress of re-homing, but will soon settle down and start laying again.

It is important to note that each egg uses 4g of calcium so your hen's caged life will have depleted her precious calcium levels. Provide her with supplements in the form of oyster shell or limestone flour.

Soft Eggs: Some ex-batts have trouble passing their eggs, especially when they are settling in as the move will have been very stressful for them. They can appear quite unwell very quickly and it can be rather frightening. A warm bath will help her expel the egg - soft eggs are difficult to expel because they have nothing to contract against unlike a hard shelled egg. Give her 2ml of Zolcal D to aid contractions. Afterwards, place her somewhere warm, quiet and dark to lay her egg. Once she has finished and if she is still damp from her bath, a blow dry (on coolest setting) can be a welcome treat! If it is a recurring problem you may need to look at a Suprelorin implant (see below).

Lash: A lash is part of the reproductive system lining that has broken away and been expelled. It can be nothing to worry about or it can indicate the end of your hen's laying days. Either way, your hen will need to be kept an eye on. It can be quite disgusting – appearing rubbery and alienlike, but try not to be too alarmed!

Two sorts of lash. Many thanks to Diana Prudhoe (left) and Vanessa Winwood (right) for their pictures. Only in chicken world would we find these fascinating!

Egg peritonitis: When a hen forms an egg it travels down the oviduct and out of the vent. Sometimes it is not caught by the oviduct and the egg fluid builds up internally in the abdominal cavity. If this becomes infected your girl can develop egg peritonitis which will most certainly need a vet's help. This is when your regular health checks become invaluable. You will notice she is getting heavier at the back end, may be sitting in the nest box but not laying and is generally off colour. She may also spend long spells sitting in the run or garden and breathing quite heavily, especially later in the day. With all my girls who have developed EP this was the first indication something was wrong.

Above: Miss Greta Garbo Chicken's swollen abdomen on rehoming. Note the shape of her abdomen compared to the more angular one of Miss Gina Chicken's which, for the purposes of this picture, is conveniently featherless! Now Greta has been treated the fluid has gone and she is left with a much less swollen mass of tissue. It is something I still check daily though.

At this point you will need a vet's intervention and you have a few options to discuss with them:

Frusemide tablets help drain away excess fluid and can thus reduce the build-up. Bunty and Greta had a quarter of a tablet once a day ground up on a treat. Be aware of the possible risk of dehydration so ensure she is drinking plenty of water.

You can have the fluid drained by the vet. This can relieve the pressure in her abdomen and she may be able to reabsorb the remaining fluid herself. There is a danger with this procedure as the sudden loss of fluid can put a strain on her heart so please be aware of this. She will have to have the antibiotic Baytril afterwards to stop any infection.

The Suprelorin implant (see P59) will stop her laying, giving her body a rest and a chance to absorb the fluid. Done early enough, this can be very successful and if you can afford it, try this.

A combination of these treatments depending on the severity of the egg peritonitis may be the best answer but as each case is different please ask your vet what they recommend.

This is also the time you do can give your girls treats and a wheat-based diet. You do not want her to lay so she can enjoy all those naughty things that are usually rationed!

Prolapse: A prolapse is when the oviduct does not immediately retract after laying and, whilst it looks quite scary, can be relatively easy to treat. It is very important to isolate your hen as red attracts unwanted pecks and could lead to a fatal bleed. Keep your hen separate until you are sure there is no chance of the prolapse recurring.

Run your girl a warm bath and add a drop of lavender essential oil. This will calm you both and will help kill any bacteria. I have also found, especially with Grace Kelly's prolapse, that it helps in shrinking it. Then clean the prolapse with Hibiscrub, and wash it with honey or sugary water, or rub in pile cream, to shrink it. Lubricate it with Vaseline and push it gently back in and hold for ten minutes. This is definitely a two person job! If it pops out, try again. If this works, isolate her until you have seen how successful your administrations have been and lubricate her vent with Vaseline each day before she lays her egg. If you are unsure about doing any of this then take her straight to the vets and if the prolapse does come out again, she will definitely need to see a vet. The vets then can put in a purse string suture to keep the prolapse in. It allows poo to pass through but not an egg so she will need daily vet checks for an impending egg. This would be the time to have an implant to stop her laying. Bunty Goodchicken had this suture and the implant and it saved her life.

Suprelorin implant: One long term solution is a Suprelorin implant, which is an injection. It will stop her laying for anything up to six months, giving her body a well-earned rest and removing the danger of further prolapses. It is not cheap, at about £60-£80, but it is a quick injection, which has proved, quite literally, a life saver for some of my girls. The old problem may return when the implant wears off so keep a very close eye on your girl when she starts to lay again.

Feathery issues

Growing Back Feathers: Ex-batts emerge from their cage in various states of featherlessness. Some have a pretty healthy set, some are almost bald but most are somewhere in between. Their feathers will soon grow back but remember that the emerging quills are very delicate. When you pick your girl up during this time, be very gentle with her as emerging feathers can be very painful .If caught they really bleed! Stem the bleeding with a little flour and then spray with purple spray.

Jumpers: Avoid chicken jumpers as these restrict that vital feather re-growth - hens are little furnaces and even in mid-winter can keep warm. Also if the jumpers get wet they can stay damp and as they are next to the skin will make the chicken cold. To keep them warm, make sure they have plenty of dry bedding, a draught free coop and a covered run. However, if, like me, you worry, explore other alternatives such as putting the coop in the greenhouse or polytunnel in mid-winter so the girls have an added layer of protection.

Wing Clipping:

Left: How to Clip a Wing

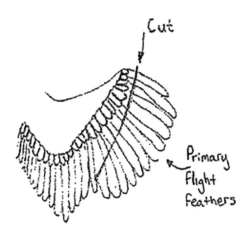

Reproduced by kind permission of http://poultrykeeper.com

There comes a time in every hen's life when the grass over the fence always seems greener! Bella was the first hen whose wing I ever clipped (I had seen the little scamp running gleefully up and down the Cornish stone wall) and I was terrified. In reality it is little more dangerous than cutting hair but definitely a two person job! Spread out one wing (only one is clipped to unbalance her) and look at the feathers. On top is a layer of smaller feathers which overlap the longer feathers underneath. You need to cut the longer, bottom feathers so they are just longer than the top layer of feathers. Use the top layer as a guide and snip each long feather. The quill will be white meaning it is dead and it will not bleed. When you get used to it you can snip away much more quickly but start off slowly!

Moult: The moult – when a hen loses many of her feathers and grows a fresh set - can take a lot out of your ex-batts, growing feathers is hard work and very painful. Poor Clara couldn't even preen herself it hurt her so much. Make sure your girl eats and drinks well and supplement her feed with something like Nettex Total Moulting Solutions which goes in her water. Ex-batts usually moult in the autumn/winter and many may moult together so they will all benefit from this supplement. Even when she has finished moulting keep it up for a month or so as her immune system will be lowered by the effort of growing her feathers. The Nettex solution is sugary (too much sugar can lead to crop problems) so after a month, put apple cider vinegar in the water for a week, then go back to the Nettex solution if needs be.

Legs

Your girls' legs may well be weak at first. A wonder treatment for this is arnica gel which can be rubbed on their legs and reduces bruising and swelling. Apply twice a day for as long as it takes – Clara, my darling girl who had spent two years in a cage and was unable to walk at all on rehoming, took a few weeks of arnica rubs to improve but was soon skipping across the garden like a...spring chicken!

Scaly Leg: This is caused by mites burrowing under her scales. As opposed to looking smooth and lying flat, they will be peeling back and flaking off. They remind me of a fungal toenail. This is easily treated, you need to spray on scaly leg treatment which is widely available and smother the legs in Vaseline. This suffocates the mites.

Bumblefoot: Caused by the staphylococcus bacterium, this is where a wound has healed over but there is pus underneath the surface. Your girl may be limping and have a very warm foot so check underneath for a scab. Soak the foot in cooled boiled water with some salt and tea tree in. If you are confident, lance the wound with a sterilised needle (put in boiling water then allowed to cool) and clean again once the pus has drained away. Put some antiseptic on the wound, cover with gauze and fix with a suitable bandage. If you are at all unsure, take your girl to the vets for them to perform this procedure. She may also need antibiotics.

Wounds

Any wounds, in particular those that are bleeding, need to be treated. Wash the wound with cooled, boiled water with some salt dissolved in it. You could also add a drop of tea tree to the water for its antiseptic properties. Then spray with purple (antiseptic spray) to deter any unwanted 'interest.'

Parasites

Worming: Flubenvet is the only licensed wormer for hens in the UK and you can eat the eggs whilst they are being treated. It is very simple to use. Each scoop (provided) is 6g. Mix this very well with 2kg of food to ensure it is evenly distributed. Your hens then need to eat this food for seven days. This kills the worm cycle. If they run out of food, make up another batch. After seven days, throw away any unused food. Check their poo during this time, you may see the odd dead worm (which looks like a bit of spaghetti). This shows the Flubenvet is working. After their initial worming, your girls will need to be wormed every three months.

Red Mite: Regular dusting with red mite powder will keep these monsters at bay. They hide in the coop during the day (in crevices and on perch edges) and come out at night and feed on the hens' blood. They look like the head of a pin and will be blackishy red, with blood coming out if you squash them. Once you have an infestation it is very hard to get rid of so prevention is better than cure. Poof Diatom in the coop as well as red mite spray in warmer weather.

Lice: These are easiest to spot around the vent and can be treated with a good louse powder. The eggs look like little white blobs at the base of the feathers close to the skin. Dust all your hens as if one has them the odds are they all will!!

Respiratory Issues

Respiratory issues in hens can show themselves as sneezing, snicking, wheezing or coughing. They are highly infectious to the rest of the flock as the disease is carried in water droplets. Your girl may have runny eyes and nostrils and her sinuses may be swollen (the pinky bits above the beak). She may also have foamy eyes which could be Mycoplasma.

Mycoplasma is potentially very serious, I lost my darling CocoChanel to Mycoplasma and it was horrible. There is a distinctive smell – sickly sweet – that indicates mycoplasma.

Whatever the respiratory complaint, she will need antibiotics from the vets. The antibiotic commonly prescribed is Baytril and for general infections this is fine. However, with respiratory infections, your hen will usually need Tylan. It is dissolved in the water so the entire flock can be treated. You may have to buy the whole tub (about £30) but dosages are small so digital scales will come in handy! Sprinkle the Tylan over the water as opposed to plopping it in. It takes a little time to dissolve so mix well. If your poorlie girl is not drinking much, ensure you syringe some of the water with Tylan into her.

Whilst your poorlie hen is recovering she can have steam inhalations. Bring her inside, wrap her in a towel and sit her on a chair – preferably on a handy lap. To a bowl of boiling water add one drop of eucalyptus oil (to clear congestion) and one of lavender (antibiotic and calming). Place this on the floor underneath the chair and waft the steam up to her. Do this two or three times a day whilst she is unwell.

If she has foamy eyes, she will be unable to clear them properly. Dip a cotton bud in warm salty water and wipe away the foam. Do this as often as necessary, every hour if needs be, with a clean bud every time.

Miss Bunty Goodchicken; covergirl, Braveheart award winner, medical pioneer and very Good Chicken. Painted by the very lovely and talented Lesley Ann Cooper.

Crop Issues

The crop is the bulgy bit at the front of the hen, which can clearly be seen here on Miss Bertha Chicken *(left)*. On a featherless girl it can look quite scary when full but it fills up with food during the day which is digested overnight and the crop is empty again in the morning.

Impacted Crop: Something - such as a long blade of grass - can get balled up in the crop and stuck. The crop will feel hard first thing in the morning. Syringe a little warm olive oil into her and massage her crop for 15 minutes at a time. Then, and this is the fun bit, feed her live maggots. They will eat away at the impaction and hopefully clear it. Drop them at the back of her throat so they go down live and whole. Lovely. Do this a few times daily and each morning feel her crop to see if the impaction has broken up. When she is starting to get better keep her diet light. Obviously if she does not respond to treatment then she needs to see a vet.

Sour Crop: This can be quite a scary thing to treat so will hopefully not happen until you are much more experienced but is worth mentioning here. If your hen has a soft full crop first thing in the morning and has foul (very foul) smelling fluid coming out of her beak, the odds are she has sour crop. You first need to clear her crop. You can hang her upside down by her feet and the fluid will fall out but it is very important you do this for a maximum of ten seconds repeated at intervals, putting her back up the right way so she can breathe each time. I found this horrifying at first so adapted it slightly. Hold your hen firmly by the body, holding in her wings as you would normally, facing her away from you, her bottom tucked into your tummy. Keeping a firm grip on her, lean as far forwards as you can so fluid tips from her beak. After clearing her crop give her an Epsom salt flush (a teaspoon of Epsom salts dissolved in a small glass of water) by syringing 5ml orally. Leave her for an hour or so - with no water or food. You can make up some critical care formula (1 tablespoon of honey, hot water, a few grains of salt and a couple of drops of citric acid) and syringe this in after an hour. Then give her a little live yoghurt with garlic in, she can have up to a heaped tablespoon per day for five days. The yoghurt replaces good bacteria and the garlic is a powerful antiseptic and antifungal treatment (sour crop is caused by candida or thrush). Take her to the vets and ask for Nystatin which is excellent for sour crop aftercare.

If, however, she has repeated sour crop or it does not clear then it may be indicative of an underlying problem so have her checked over thoroughly by your vet.

Both sour crop and impacted crop will benefit from your girl having regular apple cider vinegar in her water and a little live yoghurt and garlic occasionally.

I am not a vet so please always ask your vet's advice if you are at all unsure about your ex-batt.

Eating Eggs Whilst Your Ex-Batts are on Medication

If your vet prescribes medicines to your ex-batt they will ask you to sign a disclosure as the medicine will not be licensed for chickens. This is perfectly normal. He or she will also tell you not to eat the eggs whilst your girl is on the medication. In the case of Baytril, for example, there is a withdrawal period. What this is depends on who you speak to – some people say a week, others ten days and others just for the duration of the medicine taking.

Check with your vet as to the exact period of time. My own personal opinion is to eat the eggs anyway. The amount of antibiotic given to the ex-batt and consequently filtering through to us is so minimal, that it pales in comparison with the amount of antibiotics pumped into our food by the food manufacturers. However what you decide is obviously up to you, but if you or anyone in your family is pregnant, very young or very old or are unwell then do not eat the eggs.

You do not want to waste any eggs laid during this time by your sick girl so if you decide not to eat them, then feed them back to the ex-batts. They will love you for it!

Effie and the Implant

Effie soon after rehoming in her special ICU (converted coal hole).

Little Effie is a very special hen. She has a neck that is set at right angles – whether a birth defect or an injury I do not know. In the cage she was picked on and bullied and consequently she came to me a terrified little soul. The effects of the cages are not always limited to physical ones - Effie was emotionally traumatised by her time in them and she took months of careful nursing to even manage to go outside. She is still unable to mix with other hens but has found a friend – her first and only ever friend – in the gentle soul that is Miss Basket, who arrived with a foot so badly infected it was black and hung lifelessly. Both girls are now much better and have the free run of the half of the garden set aside for humans (ha! The best laid plans...) and live a life of sunbathing, worm hunting and cuddles.

Unwell Effie decides cuddles with her mum are just what a sick girl needs.

But our time together when Effie was recovering means we have a very special bond. We share a special language. I know when she is happy or sad, grumpy or feeling ill, whether she wants a cuddle or wants to be left alone. She, in turn, instinctively knows when I am sad and always tries her best to comfort me – allowing me an extra long cuddle.

So one night I knew that my Effie was unwell. As opposed to her normal scurrying headlong towards the mealworms, she stood still, her head tilted to one side, looking at me with those big, beautiful eyes. When it comes to illness Effie doesn't cope too well. She is a mummy's girl.

She was brewing a soft egg. She came inside for a warm bath, some Zolcal D and cuddles. She climbed onto my shoulder and fell asleep, nestled into my hair. She spent the night tucked up with a cuddly toy in Tom's room.

Once the egg made its appearance Effie was much improved and scuttled off outside to tell Miss Basket of her adventures. However, more soft eggs were to follow so Effie was taken to Uncle Jason the vet for a Suprelorin implant.

I was very worried about her reaction to the injection (it's a big needle) but after an hour of love and fuss and a little scrambled egg, she was bright as a button, hungry and ready to go outside to see Miss Basket. She was egg free for over four months and on her return to laying has produced a perfect egg every day.

It's a big world for a little hen.

Miss CocoChanel Chicken

CHAPTER 7

Saying Goodbye to Your Girls

Note: Normally in hen-keeping guides there is now a 'how to dispatch your chicken' section which I studiously avoid. I would not dispatch my cat if she was ill, so nor would I attempt to dispatch my chicken. Ex-batts are pets, they are rehomed as pets and I treat my girls as part of the family. To me the only responsible way for your girl's life to end is naturally in her sleep or at the hands of a vet. This is an emotional chapter in parts and I make no apologies for that.

Left: Miss Brigit Chicken's memorial stone.

Losing any family pet is a sad and emotional time but losing one of your ex-batt girls can be even worse. Every day they can spend out of the cage, being 'real' chickens, is a good day and when they die before their time, missing out on all that free range happiness, it is truly heartbreaking. Doubly so if they have spent longer in the cage than out of it. Fate dealt our girls a very rough hand initially; we can only hope that after their free range life, they passed away with only memories of sunshine, freedom and love, their former lives long forgotten.

However, whenever your girl passes on and however she passes on it is never easy. One part of me hopes that if it is their time that they will drift away in their sleep, gently, peacefully and with their sisters around them. It is not always like that though.

Putting Your Girl to Sleep

As an ex-batt owner, making the decision to put your hen to sleep is the hardest one of all. Torn between wanting to try everything to save her and not wanting her to suffer - making the correct decision for your girl is soul wrenching. However, when you have sat with her in your arms, stroked her feathers, soothed her, dug up your best veg beds to find tasty worms to tempt her, given her medicine, let her know how much you love her and walked in the sunshine cuddling her so she can feel the sun on her feathers one last time, you will know when it is time. Your girl will let you know when she is ready to go. Remember always that any decision you do make is made out of love.

Left: Tom's hen Evie, a poorlie girl from a rehoming day. She enjoyed a few months of sunshine and freedom before her brave little heart gave out.

On that last difficult journey to the vet I refuse to put her in any sort of cage, be it a cat carrier or box; my girls' last memories will not be of the inside of a cage.

I wrap her in the softest towel we have so she feels safe and warm and ask my husband to drive us to the vets. Keeping her in my arms at all times, the vet will check her over and agree with me we are making the right decision. We are blessed with a very gentle and knowledgeable vet who, after injecting my girl, will leave us alone in the room with her as she passes. And it is a gentle process.

I have lost a few girls this way and they do just fall asleep. I cradle them and stroke their feathers and talk to them the whole time. Hearing is the last sense to go and I am sure they die knowing they are loved. It is little comfort to us humans but I am sure it helps the hen pass more peacefully and at the end of the day they are what is important.

Saying Goodbye to Your Girl

Remember also that if you lose an ex-batt, your other girls will grieve for her too. They will have seen her become unwell and her closest friends will have nursed her during her illness. Unless they are with her when she goes they will not understand where she has gone. It was Grace Kelly's alarm call that alerted us to Gina's passing away – hens understand what is happening and their feelings must be taken into account at this terrible time. When we lost Bunty Goodchicken and Clara in close succession, their friend Bella was off colour for days. She used to climb onto my lap and nestle down, she used to take herself off into a corner and she used to look for them at bedtime.

Our first three hens – Audrey, Agatha and Aurora – were buried in the garden, under the hydrangea. They were a flock in life and it was important they remained a flock in death. Each girl has their own grave with a stone, picked from Portreath beach, and decorated with their name, hearts and flowers. Poignantly, the previously pink hydrangea flowers turned blue the first summer the girls lay under there. I like to think they are still with us, enjoying the sun with their younger sisters and watching their antics.

However, burying hens in your garden is actually illegal as the wise sparks at Defra still class chickens as livestock and not pets. But it was not this questionable ruling that changed our burial practices but a more practical reason: our garden is not large and we were going to be having many hens over the years. So now we cremate our deceased girls and then bury their ashes.

The Practicalities

Our cremations are done at dusk, after the other girls have gone to bed. We have converted an old oil drum *(above)* and cut a large hole (chicken shaped) for decoration really but also for airflow and lots of small holes (8-10 mm in diameter) in vertical rows down the sides near the bottom to get air flow circulating. We use dry, fast burning wood, usually old pallets or pine which are chopped up and stored in the garage just for this purpose.

The first batch of wood is burnt using an accelerant such as white spirit to ensure it gets really hot. Then a second batch of wood is burnt and once that has got going, a flat section in the wood is made and the hen put in. She is wrapped up in something soft to keep her warm. I am currently using some pink material with flowers on that I have cut up into chicken blanket sized pieces which is suitably pretty and feminine. A spade is the safest way to lower her gently into the flames. We also place a flower, special to the girl, in with her. Miss Constance Chicken (above), for example, always liked to sit in between the pond and the big white flowers, so when we cremated her, I placed some of these white flowers in with her. She was also quite a whiffy girl in life due to her bottom issues so I also put some rosemary in with her to make sure that she smelled beautiful. I think she would have appreciated it.

The fire is stoked to keep it very hot and a third load of wood added to keep it burning for another hour or so. Then the embers will do the rest. Overnight it will finish off and by the morning there will be just ash and maybe the odd small bone but nothing nasty. There is also no smell at all.

There is something rather comforting about watching the flames flicker up towards the heavens, almost as if your girl's spirit is soaring up to the stars. The small ventilation holes flicker gently like stars as we say goodbye to our angel. That evening we also burn candles for her and remember all the sisters she is joining and flying free with.

Once cold we bury the ashes in a large pot submerged in the garden, next to the A girls' graves, and cover it with a large, heavy stone. As with the A girls, each girl has a stone, picked from Portreath beach, and decorated with her name, hearts and flowers and placed on the grave. Each morning, the hens and I talk to them. I find it a comfort and I am sure they do as well. Hens grieve as we do and I am certain on some level they know that their sisters are still with us.

Vets also offer a cremation service but I like to see the whole journey through from taking her out of the cage, watching her grow into a strong happy free range hen, enjoying being part of her new life, nursing her when she needs me and ultimately seeing her safely off on her final journey. A vet cremation service can vary from approximately £30 up to about £90 for an individual cremation. Please ask at your vets for more information about this.

Fly High Little Hens

What we must try to remember is that every day these girls spend out of the cage is a good day. Every day they can forage and scratch and spread their wings, every day they can dustbathe and preen and sunbathe, chase flies and hunt for worms. Every day they can do all these things is a good day, be it for just one day or for many months or many years. When they are ill, they are nursed, loved and cared for and when they die they are surrounded by their sisters or cradled in the arms of their loving owners. They are buried with dignity and grieved for. They were the lucky ones. Hundreds of thousands of their sisters live in cages and die in fear. No-one buries them and no-one grieves for them. They have no name, no identity, no dignity and never knew what it was like to spend their days in the sun or feel the love and kindness some humans can give them. As ex-battery hen owners we are fighting against the physical and emotional scars that intensive farming inflicts on our poor hens. It is a battle we cannot win but we can rescue as many hens as we can and surround them with the love they so deserve. Which brings me back to the quote from the first chapter of the book:

Saving one hen won't change the world,
but it will change the world for that hen.

Miss Audrey Chicken

CHAPTER 8

Frequently Asked Questions

Do ex-batts lay eggs?
Yes! The hens are sent to slaughter when they are no longer commercially viable that is, laying an egg a day. Ex-batts will still lay, after a possible initial settling in period. Obviously you are never guaranteed eggs but on average I would say you would get four eggs a week from an ex-batt. Egg laying, as with all hens, slows down during the winter months and starts again in the spring.

Do you need a cockerel to have eggs?
No. Hens lay eggs regardless of whether there is a cockerel there or not.

Why don't you have a cockerel?
Firstly in consideration to our neighbours, although I love to hear their crowing in the morning, our lovely neighbour Pat might not be so keen. Secondly cockerels can get very amorous and I think my girls have had more than enough to put up with in their short lives. The last thing they need is some randy bloke jumping all over them! And lastly, a cockerel would mean fertilised eggs which as a vegetarian I would not be happy to eat. The worry of hatched eggs and what to do with any male chicks is also

something I do not want to deal with.

Do hens attract rats?
Hens do not attract rats but their food might do. Ensure all food is taken up at the end of the day and keep food preparation areas clean. Put bags or sacks of food in containers such as plastic bins that cannot be gnawed through. I have never had a rat problem and it is not something that is a big concern.

Can I give them treats?
Treats should be just that! A treat. Give them mash during the day and when they have filled up on mash, which they require to get sufficient nutrients to lay, give them some treats in the late afternoon. Treats make them put on weight and obese hens do not lay eggs. Ideal treats are mealworms, corn (especially during cold nights as it helps keep them warm), greens and seeds.

Can I feed them kitchen scraps?
To me, an important aspect of hen keeping is that you are a little bit self-sufficient and are being environmentally conscious. It makes sense to feed your hens scraps from the kitchen - it is something that was universally done in days gone by and prevents waste. What better use of some leftover supper than to feed it to your hens in the afternoon as part of their treats? They convert it into delicious eggs or highly efficient fertiliser. However, those bright sparks at Defra cannot differentiate between my pet chickens and a farmer with 20,000 hens in a shed. Their blanket rule states hens cannot be fed food from the kitchen. I could not possibly encourage you to break this law...it is entirely your decision!

What happens if my hens eat their eggs?
In the farm the hens will never have seen their eggs so in their new free range lives they will undoubtedly enjoy sitting on them for a little while having a little post-laying contemplate. In my years of ex-batt keeping I have only ever had one girl eat the eggs,

Miss Basket aka the Phantom Egg Eater of Old Camborne town!
Whilst my initial reaction was to try to stop her eating eggs, upon reflection I came to a decision. It was, after all, her egg so why should she not enjoy it?
You may have noticed I spoil my girls a tad but I do agree with the idea that the chicken owns the egg she lays. My girls are pets, eggs are just a bonus after all.

Above: Miss Basket aka the Phantom Egg Eater!

So now there is an egg hierarchy in our house that goes: poorly chicken, any chicken that wants it, humans. But in all seriousness if you do have an egg eater and you want to stop her try to get to the eggs first or try the mustard in the empty egg trick. I have never tried it but have heard that it works!

Will the hens be OK in very cold weather? Even if they have no feathers?
Cold weather will stimulate feather growth. In very cold weather, though, try to keep any featherless girls inside in a stable, barn or greenhouse to give them a little protection from the elements. Feathered hens are OK down to minus 10c but ensure they have plenty of dry bedding and a draught free coop, and give them warm mash to help keep them toasty. That said, when it is very cold I do bring my girls inside to warm up. I also cover their coops with something to insulate them such a newspaper and a blanket, bubble wrap or tarpaulin. I have stopped short of hot water bottle. So far.

Can I put food and water bowls in the coop with them?
Generally no. It will not do any harm but they will undoubtedly spill the water over the bedding. Keep food and drink in the run!

If, however, you have a poorlie girl who is in the coop, then ensure she has access to food and water in the coop.

How long do ex-batts live for?
That is really the same as asking how long is piece of string. When you get your girls, they will have been in the farm for about 18 months. They will have gone in at point of lay so will be about two years old. Non-commercial hens can live for many years but in all honesty and from my experience and that of my ex-batty friends I would say your girls will live with you for an average of about two years. Some may live less than that, some may live a lot longer. Every day you spend with them is a privilege.

Why do you take on sick girls?
Because they are the most precious! Just as I would always go for the runt of the litter, so I would always take on a poorlie girl. The healthy hens go to the rehomers and as a co-ordinator it is my job to nurse the poorlies back to health. Very occasionally these poorlie girls are very sick but as my literary hero Atticus Finch, in To Kill a Mockingbird, said: "It's when you know you're licked before you begin but you begin anyway and you see it through no matter what. You rarely win, but sometimes you do."

How important is giving your girl a name?
Absolutely vital! A name means your hen is an individual, it acknowledges she has her own character, it shows she is special and has her own little space on this planet and it gives her dignity! So many hens die with no name and no dignity - your girls need to make up for that!

What can I do if I can't have hens?
If you cannot have hens of your own, you can still help ex-batts. As campaigns such as Chicken Out have shown, the British public care deeply about animal welfare; what they lack are truthful and accurate facts so they can make an informed decision.

Whilst UK farmers are all compliant with the barren cage ban, some EU countries (most notably Italy Poland, Greece and Spain) still defy the law and have the old-style barren cages. The UK government did not support its own farmers and thus failed to ban the import of these now illegal eggs. Whilst it is easy to identify barren caged shelled eggs (due to unique markings seen under ultraviolet), it is impossible to trace the source of liquid egg which is widely used in commercial products. Eggs crop up in no end of products, from the obvious quiches and pies to less obvious products such as wine. To ensure your eggs are not from illegal barren cages make sure the label says free range.

The only way to make the egg industry and the supermarkets listen to us is not to buy caged eggs. Or colony eggs. Or whatever the new marketing word for caged is. Always buy free range eggs. And always check the ingredients list of any manufactured products for egg. If it doesn't say 'free range' it most certainly won't be. Then tell companies and supermarkets why you are not buying caged eggs.

Free range eggs currently make up 50% of the market. It is up to us to make sure they are soon 100%.

Miss Gina Chicken enjoys the sun on her feathers – for the first time in her life.

Miss Grace Kelly Chicken

CHAPTER 9

Other Useful Information

Hen Rehoming Charities

British Hen Welfare Trust **http://www.bhwt.org.uk/**

Free at Last **http://free-at-last.org.uk/**

Fresh Start for Hens **http://www.freshstartforhens.co.uk/**

Little Hen Rescue
http://www.littlehenrescue.co.uk/Pages/default.aspx

Lucky Hen Rescue
http://luckyhensrescuenorthwest.weebly.com/

Northern Ireland Hen rescue
http://www.nuthousehenrescue.co.uk/Home.html

RSPCA **http://www.rspca.org.uk/home**

Wing and a Prayer Rescue:
http://www.facebook.com/WingAndAPrayerRescue

Useful Websites

For more information, stories and photos of my beautiful ex-batts including the international celebrity that is Effie, please visit my blog: **http://lifewiththeexbatts.wordpress.com/**

Poultrykeeper **http://poultrykeeper.com/** For all things chicken with an excellent ex-batt section and poultry forum.

Allotment **http://www.allotment.org.uk/**   Useful website and home of the infamous Poo Picture (p52) which they very kindly let me use.

Avian   Vets   **http://avianveterinaryservices.co.uk/index.html** Excellent chicken vet in the North West.

Chicken Vet **http://www.chickenvet.co.uk/**   Chicken health advice and information and stockists of specialist supplies.

Compassion in World Farming **http://www.ciwf.org.uk/**   The farm animal welfare charity.

Chicken Out: **http://www.chickenout.tv/** Campaigning for a free range future.

Green Living Forum
http://www.thegreenlivingforum.net/forum/index.php For a wealth of information on living a greener life. Large livestock and poultry section.

Janet Jamieson Art **https://www.facebook.com/pages/Janets-Chicken-Art**   Beautiful chicken portraits

Lesley Cooper Art
https://www.facebook.com/LesleyAnnsChickenArt Beautiful chicken portraits

Smallholder magazine **http://www.smallholder.co.uk/** Large poultry section each month.

The Poultry Pages **http://www.poultry.allotment.org.uk/** Chicken information and forum

Your Chickens **http://www.yourchickens.co.uk/home** Website for pet chicken keepers. Also a monthly magazine.

Stockists

Amazon **https://www.amazon.co.uk/** For coops and supplies.

Cluck Buddy Coops **http://www.cluckbuddy.com/** Recycled plastic coops for ex-batts.

Flytes so Fancy **http://www.flytesofancy.co.uk/index.html** For coops and supplies.

Oakdene Coops **http://www.oakdene-coops.co.uk/Home.html** For plastic coops.

Wells Poultry **http://www.chicken-house.co.uk/** For coops and supplies.

Miss Flavia Chicken

Not all rescue hens are ex-batts! Miss Flavia Chicken was abandoned at the vet after a dog attack. They asked us if we would have her. As if we would say no! Exotic and beautiful, she is a Black Rock and named after our favourite Strictly dancer!

Index

ABOUT THE AUTHOR

Jo is lucky enough to live in west Cornwall with her wonderful family, many beautiful ex-battery hens and six rescue cats! She writes extensively about her girls in magazines, on websites and in her blog: http://lifewiththeexbatts.wordpress.com/

Printed in Great Britain
by Amazon.co.uk, Ltd.,
Marston Gate.